To Gail,
Enjoy nature,
Sally Fine

Hearts in Nature

Hearts in Nature

by Sally Fine

DORRANCE PUBLISHING CO., INC.
PITTSBURGH, PENNSYLVANIA 15222

ISBN-10 # 0-8059-7058-4
ISBN-13 # 978-0-8059-7058-6
Printed in the United States of America

First Printing

For information or to order additional books, please write:
Dorrance Publishing Co., Inc.
701 Smithfield Street
Third Floor
Pittsburgh; Pennsylvania 15222
U.S.A.
1-800-788-7654
Or visit our web site and on-line catalog at
www.dorrancebookstore.com

Hearts
In
Nature
COMPILED BY - SALLY FINE
PHOTOGRAPHS - SALLY FINE

" I am seeking, I am striving, I am in it with all my heart."

Vincent Van Gogh
(30 March 1853 - 29 July 1890)

Come walk with me in the woods,
  and enjoy the beauty that abounds.
Delight in the pleasures you see,
  look closer at natures bounty.
Hear the sounds of the woods,
  let them speak to your inner being.
Rejoice in the smell of the air,
  let it swell within bringing happiness.
Become one with the earth you walk on,
  have peace and inner tranquility.
Come walk with me in the woods.

May your heart soar with
love for the beauty that
beckons outside your doorstop.

Gall

A growth that is caused by fungi, bacteria or insects. Galls have a rough irregular surface. Galls can turn foliage yellow, slow growth and generally weaken a tree.

My love is like to ice

My love is like to ice, and I to fire:
How comes it then that this her cold so great
Is not dissolved through my so hot desire,
But harder grows the more I her entreat?
Or how comes it that my exceeding heat
Is not allayed by her heart-frozen cold,
But that I burn much more in boiling sweat,
And feel my flames augmented manifold?
What more miraculous thing may be told,
That fire, which all things melts, should harden ice,
And ice, which is congealed with senseless cold,
Should kindle fire by wonderful device?
Such is the power of love in gentle mind,
That it can alter all the course of kind.

Edmund Spenser
(c. 1552 - 16 January 1599)

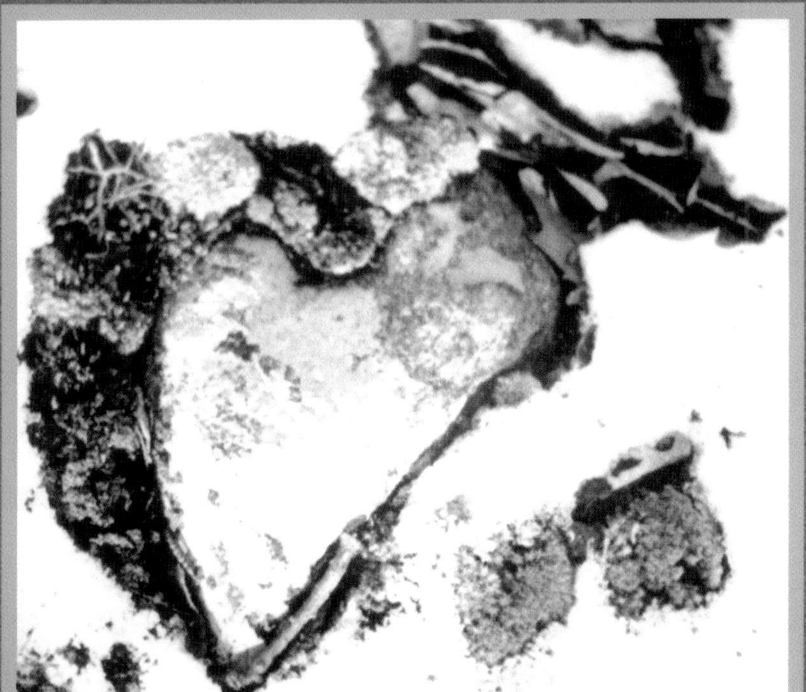

My Dear Mistress Has a Heart

My dear mistress has a heart
Soft as those kind looks she gave me,
When with love's resistless art,
And her eyes, she did enslave me;
But her constancy's so weak,
She's so wild and apt to wander,
That my jealous heart would break
Should we live one day asunder.

Melting joys about her move,
Killing pleasures, wounding blisses;
She can dress her eyes in love,
And her lips can arm with kisses;
Angels listen when she speaks,
She's my delight, all mankind's wonder;
But my jealous heart would break
Should we live one day asunder.

John Wilmot
(1647 - 1680)

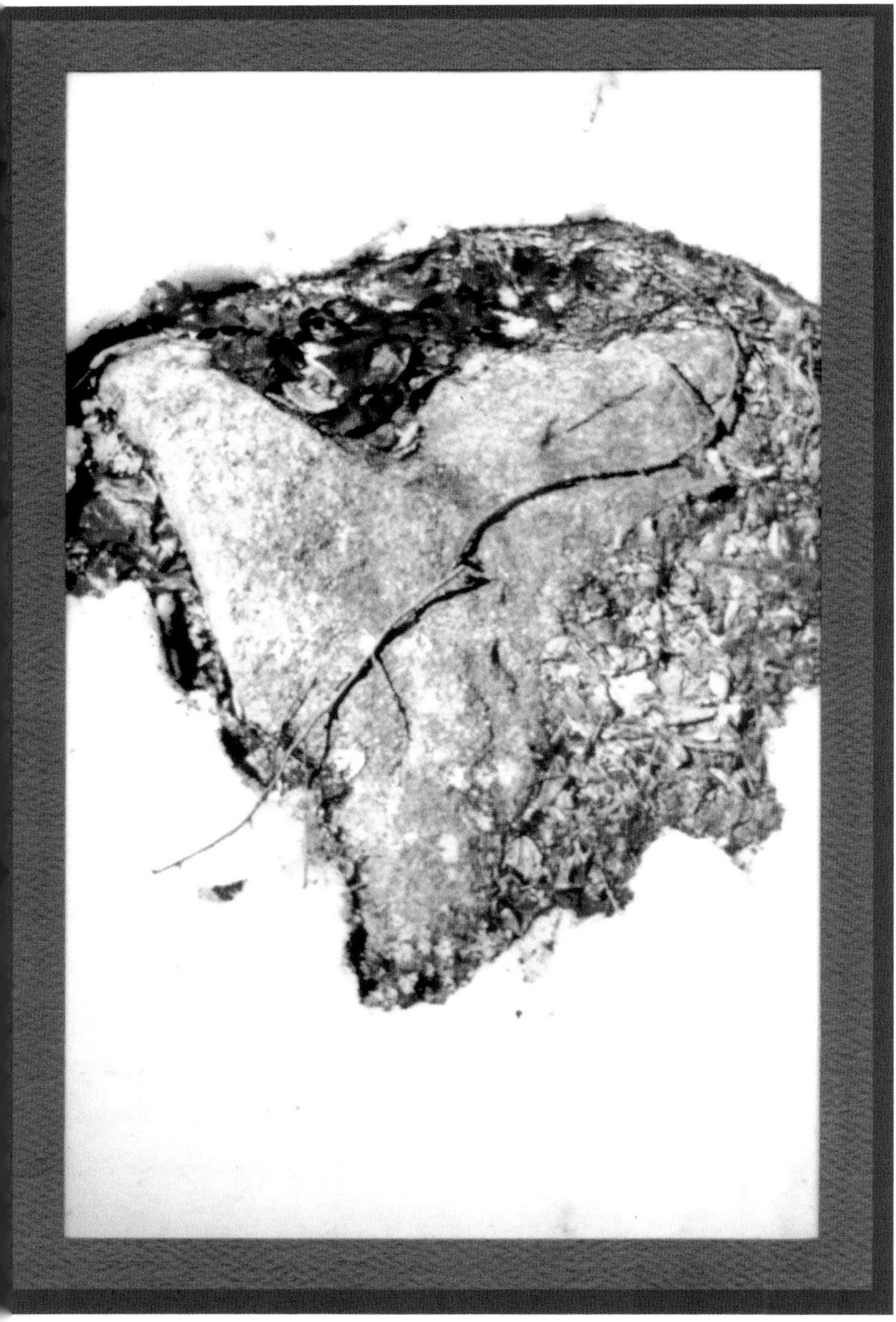

Shadow

Connected in my mind, always there,
An image to ponder.
Attached in feeling, wanting you close,
Echoing of vibrations.
A friend to talk to, relieving sorrows,
Encouraging with smiles and laughter.
A warm spot, blanketing me,
Ready for the next adventure.
Suddenly gone, emptiness a void,
Incapable of filling.
A shadow, my love lost,
But never to be forgotten.

Natures paintbrush
touching earth with love.
Its heart encompassed by
a snowy blanket.
A fleeting glimpse at a
sight to behold.

Follow your heart and let your dreams come true.

Love hath a language
of his own.
A voice that goes
from heart to heart—
whose mystic tone
love only knows.

Anon, Persian Love Poem

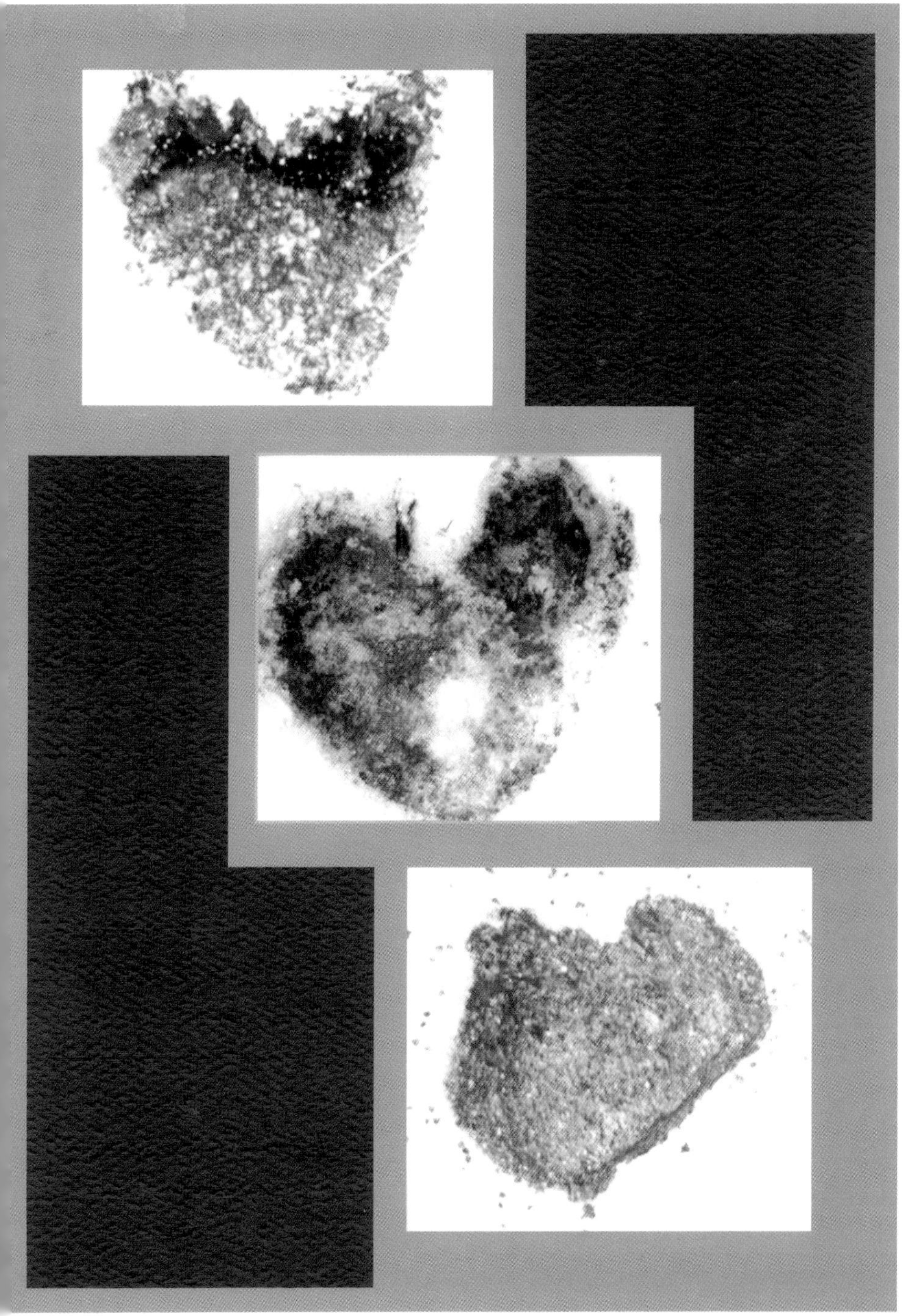

From "The Prelude"

The bliss of walking daily in
life's prime.
Through field or forest with the
maid we love.
While yet our hearts are young,
while yet we breathe
nothing but happiness.

William Wordsworth
1770-1850

I am yours,
you are mine.
Of this we are certain.
You are lodged in my heart,
the small key is lost.
You must stay there forever.

Frau Ava 12th Century
trs from The German
By Willis Barnstone

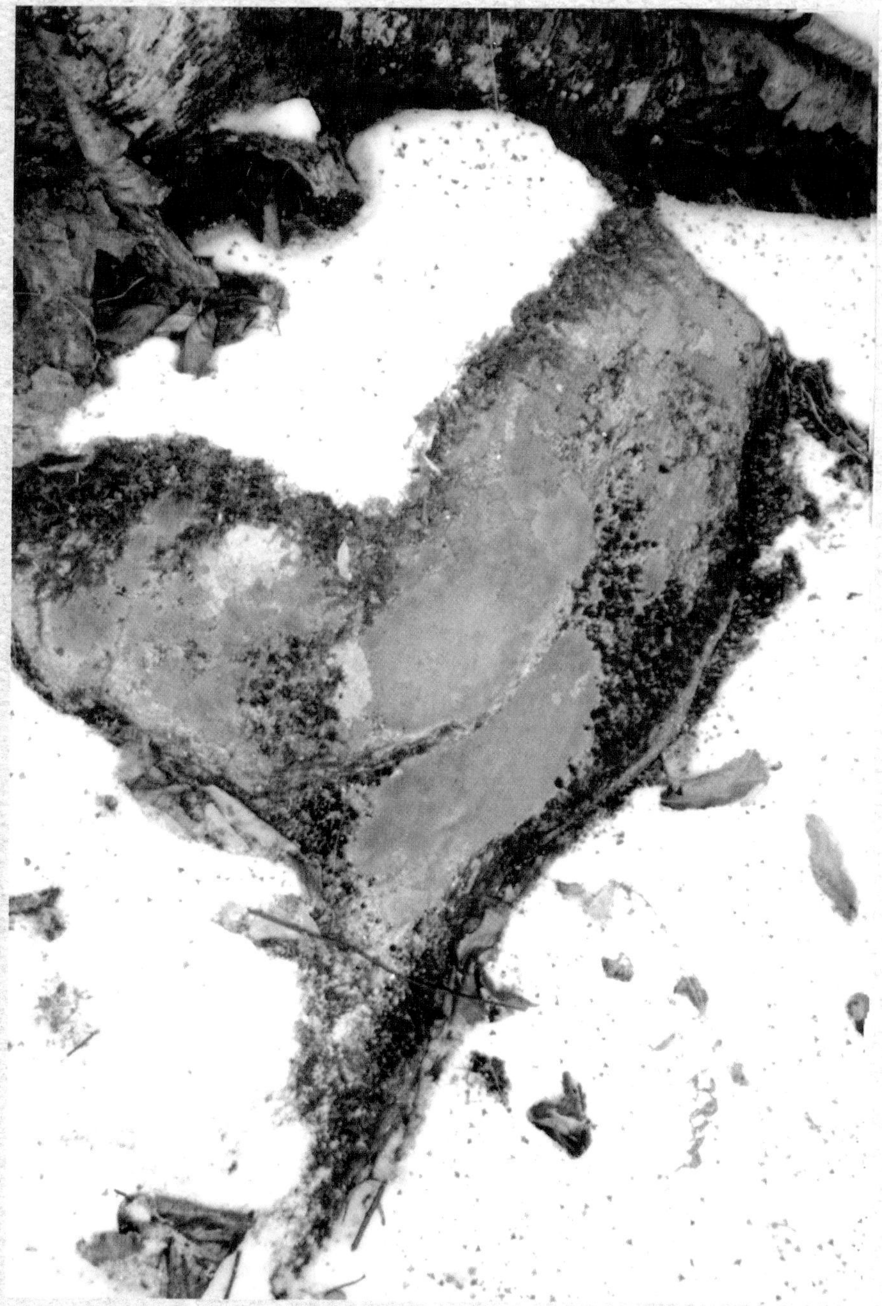

Love

Love bade me welcome; yet my soul drew back,
  Guilty of dust and sin.
But quick-eyed Love, observing me grow slack
  From my first entrance in,
Drew nearer to me, sweetly questioning
  If I lack'd anything.

'A guest,' I answer'd, 'worthy to be here':
  Love said, 'You shall be he.'
'I, the unkind, ungrateful? Ah, my dear,
  I cannot look on Thee.'
Love took my hand and smiling did reply,
  'Who made the eyes but I?'

'Truth, Lord: but I have marr'd them: let my shame
  Go where it doth deserve.'
'And know you not,' says Love, 'Who bore the blame?'
  'My dear, then I will serve.'
'You must sit down,' says Love, 'and taste my meat.'
  So I did sit and eat.

George Herbert
(3 April 1593 – 3 March 1633)

Sonnet 116

Let me not to the marriage of true minds
Admit impediments. Love is not love
Which alters when it alteration finds,
Or bends with the remover to remove:
Oh no, it is an ever fixèd mark
That looks on tempests and is never shaken;
It is the star to every wandering bark,
Whose worth's[1] unknown, although his height[2] be taken.
Love's not Time's fool, though rosy lips and cheeks
Within his bending sickle's compass come;
Love alters not with his brief hours and weeks,
But bears it out even to the edge of doom.
  If this be error and upon me proved,
  I never writ, nor no man ever loved.

William Shakespeare
(23 April 1564 - 23 April 1616)

Nature does nothing uselessly.

Aristotle
(384 BC - 322 BC)

Love is love

The lowest trees have tops, the ant her gall,
The fly her spleen, the little spark his heat:
The slender hairs cast shadows, though but small,
And bees have stings, although they be not great;
  Seas have their source, and so have shallow springs;
  And love is love, in beggars and in kings.

Where waters smoothest run, there deepest are the fords,
The dial stirs, yet none perceives it move;
The firmest faith is found in fewest words,
The turtles do not sing, and yet they love;
  True hearts have ears and eyes, no tongues to speak;
  They hear and see, and sigh, and then they break.

Sir Edward Dyer
(ca. 1543 - May 1607)

The rain came, leaving its
    mark of my love for you.
Wet and warm, tumbling down,
    carving a heart in rivets of
    stone.
Replaced quickly by glistening
    sunshine.
A moment of pleasure for me
    alone.

The Silent Lover

Passions are liken'd best to floods and streams:
The shallow murmer, but the deep are dumb;
So, when affection yields discourse, it seems
The bottom is but shallow whence they come.
They that are rich in words, in words discover
That they are poor in that which makes a lover.

Sir Walter Raleigh
(1552 - 1618)

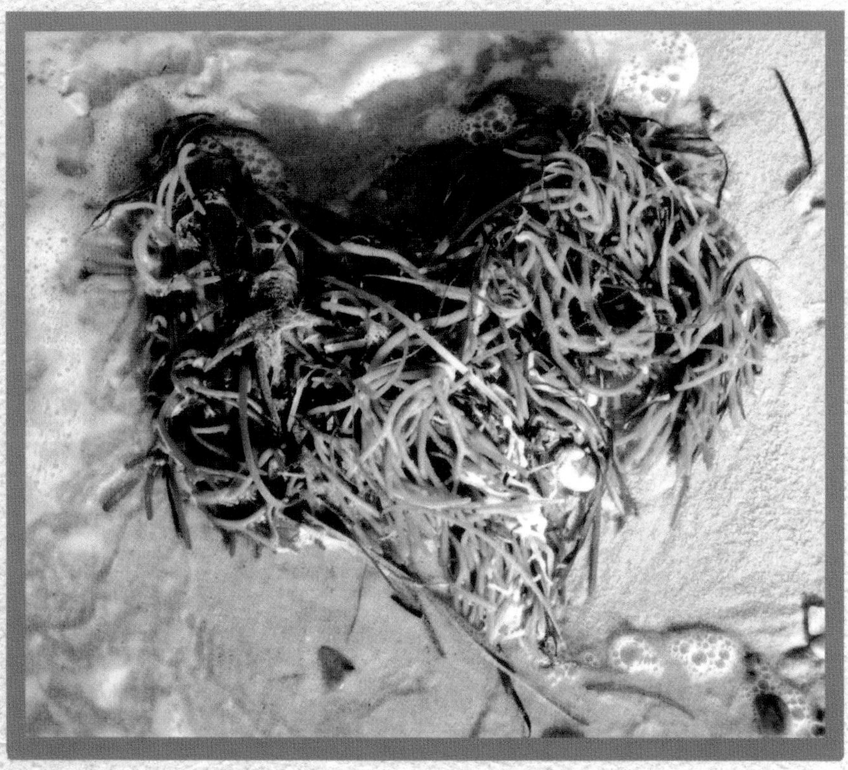

My love is like a red red rose

My love is like a red red rose
That's newly sprung in June:
My love is like the melody
That's sweetly play'd in tune.

As fair art thou, my bonnie lass,
So deep in love am I:
And I will love thee still, my dear,
Till a' the seas gang dry.

Till a' the seas gang dry, my dear,
And the rocks melt wi' the sun:
And I will love thee still, my dear,
While the sands o' life shall run.

And fare thee weel, my only love,
And fare thee weel a while!
And I will come again, my love,
Tho' it were ten thousand mile.

Robert Burns

(25 January 1759 - 21 July 1796)

Love's philosophy

The fountains mingle with the river
  And the rivers with the Ocean,
The winds of Heaven mix for ever
  With a sweet emotion;
Nothing in the world is single;
  All things by a law divine
In one spirit meet and mingle.
  Why not I with thine ? –

See the mountains kiss high Heaven
  And the waves clasp one another;
No sister-flower would be forgiven
  If it disdained its brother;
And the sunlight clasps the earth
  And the moonbeams kiss the sea:
What is all this sweet work worth
  If thou kiss not me ?

Percy Bysshe Shelley
(4 August 1792 – 8 July 1822)

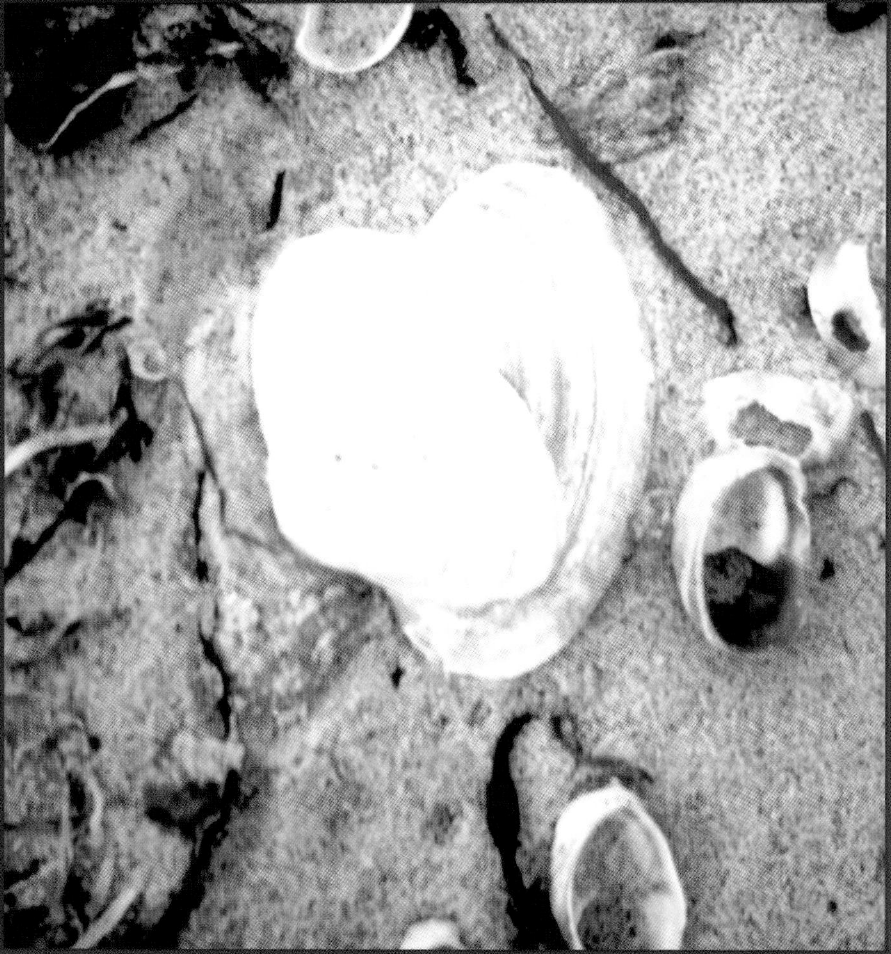

Heartbeat

Waves tumbling, a constant motion,
A rhythemic pattern, never broken.
Forcing forward, a possible menace,
Spray and foam, a visual delight.
Internal strength, the sound of power,
Not unlike the beat of your heart.

My Heart Leaps Up When I Behold

My heart leaps up when I behold
A rainbow in the sky:
So was it when my life began,
So is it now I am a man,
So be it when I shall grow old
Or let me die!
The child is father of the man:
And I could wish my days to be
Bound each to each by natural piety.

William Wordsworth
(1770 - 1850)

Sonnet Number 18

Shall I compare thee to a summer's day?
Thou art more lovely and more temperate:
Rough winds do shake the darling buds of May,
And summer's lease hath all too short a date;
Sometime too hot the eye of heaven shines,
And often is his gold complexion dimmed;
And every fair from fair sometime declines,
By chance or nature's changing course untrimmed:
But thy eternal summer shall not fade,
Nor lose possession of that fair thou ow'st,
Nor shall death brag thou wand'rest in his shade,
When in eternal lines to time thou grow'st.
So long as men can breathe or eyes can see,
So long lives this, and this gives life to thee.

William Shakespeare
(23 April 1564 - 23 April 1616)

A morning glory at my window
satisfies me more than the
metaphysic of books.

Walt Whitman
(1819 - 1892)

Garden Wall

I gaze along my garden wall
  looking for secret places.
Where spiders weave their works of art,
  shimmering in sunlight's embraces.
Twigs stick out for birds to snatch
  to create nests for their young.
The ivy grasps tenaciously, for
  spring has begun.
The wall surrounds a special place
  where hours I've spent tending.
Plots of dirt that will give forth
  flowers never ending.
Riots of color I've planted,
  with each having its own space.
To fill a void with a certain hue,
  and its own definite shape.
As days unfold and my garden grows,
  hours are spent assisting.
Keeping weeds from tiny plants whose
  tender stems are reaching.
Soft dew and gentle light slowly
  warm the earth,
Making the ground warm and anxious
  for rebirth.
The gardens where you can come
  to sit or recline.
The gardens a place to have great thoughts,
  or relax and ease the mind.
The garden's work stems from
  the heart,
Emerging into a work of art.

How do I love thee? let me count the ways

How do I love thee? Let me count the ways.
I love thee to the depth and breadth and height
My soul can reach, when feeling out of sight
For the ends of being and ideal grace.
I love thee to the level of every day's
Most quiet need, by sun and candlelight.
I love thee freely, as men strive for right;
I love thee purely, as they turn from praise.
I love thee with the passion put to use
In my old griefs, and with my childhood's faith.
I love thee with a love I seemed to lose
With my lost saints – I love thee with the breath,
Smiles, tears, of all my life! – and, if God choose,
I shall but love thee better after death.

Elizabeth Barrett Browning
(6 March 1806 - 29 June 1861)

OKALIS

A common weed also referred to as yellow woodsorrel or sourgrass. The weed usually grows in well maintained areas. The leaves contain oxalic acid which causes a sour taste.

I marvel at the way you walk.
I shudder when you talk.
You stole my heart with ease,
And left me on my knees.
I no longer know what to say.
You have taken my words away.
I pledge my heart to you,
With three words, "I love you."

Morgan Fine

Chariot Of Love

On the chariot of my soul I ride,
I am the understanding horseman,
And I hold the reins of the two horses that pull.
Both are strong and beautiful,
Pulling the chariot with swift speed.
One is pure white,
The other ebony black.
The white is obedient in his pursuit of honor.
He maintains a steady pace,
A constant speed driven by truth.
The black is more difficult.
His sexual desire makes him wild,
And his pace is erratic and unpredictable.
It is when the charioteer has control of both,
That the soul in love has balance.
It is the balance that is sought after by all.
It is the balance that I have achieved for you.
I am the charioteer in control,
Whose undying love I maintain for you.

Morgan Fine

Sonnet Number 22

My glass shall not persuade me I am old
So long as youth and thou are of one date,
But when in thee time's furrows I behold,
Then look I death my days should expiate.
For all that beauty that doth cover thee
Is but the seemly raiment of my heart,
Which in thy breast doth live, as thine in me.
How can I then be elder than thou art?
O therefore love, be of thyself so wary
As I not for myself, but for thee will,
Bearing thy heart, which I will keep so chary
As tender nurse her babe from faring ill.
Presume not on thy heart when mine is slain,
Thou gav'st me thine not to give back again.

William Shakespeare
(23April 1564 - 23 April 1616)

**To see a world in a
grain of sand,
and a heaven in a
wild flower,
hold infinity in the
palm of your hand,
and eternity in an
hour.**

William Blake
(1757 - 1827)

Sonnet Number 19

Devouring time, blunt thou the lion's paws,
And make the earth devour her own sweet brood;
Pluck the keen teeth from the fierce tiger's jaws,
And burn the long-lived phoenix in her blood;
Make glad and sorry seasons as thou fleet'st
And do whate'er thou wilt, swift-footed time,
To the wide world and all her fading sweets;
But I forbid thee one most heinous crime,
O carve not with thy hours my love's fair brow,
Nor draw no lines there with thine ántique pen.
Him in thy course untainted do allow,
For beauty's pattern to succeeding men.
Yet do thy worst, old time; despite thy wrong,
My love shall in my verse ever live young.

William Shakespeare
(23 April 1564 - 23 April 1616)

Nature never did betray the heart that loved her.

William Wordsworth
(1770 - 1850)

Peppered

Sweet,
Hot,
Tangy,
Zestful,
You've peppered my life
With love

In all things of nature there
is something of the marvelous.

Aristotle
(384 BC - 322 BC)

My heart quakes in anticipation.
The caress of the wind,
  the warmth of the sun
  embodying my soul.
I wait until our hearts intertwine.
Our love everlasting,
  at peace together,
  now and forever.

Silence

Our hearts have turned to stone.
We no longer desire each other.
Our days of love are in the past.
When time was spent together.

Tic tic tic, it's racing,
Tic tic tic, please stop,
Tic tic tic, ever forward,
Racing with the clock.

Schedules to be met,
Tasks to be done,
Errands never ending,
Forever on the run,

Dashing besides each other,
Never resting to stop.
We are always racing,
Racing with the clock,

Falling in our bed,
Attempting a good sleep,
Maybe tomarrow,
That appointment we will keep.

Silence came on slowly,
We hardly noticed at all.
We were so busy racing,
With the clock on the wall.

Our hearts have turned to stone.
We no longer desire each other.
The days of love are in the past.
When time was spent together.

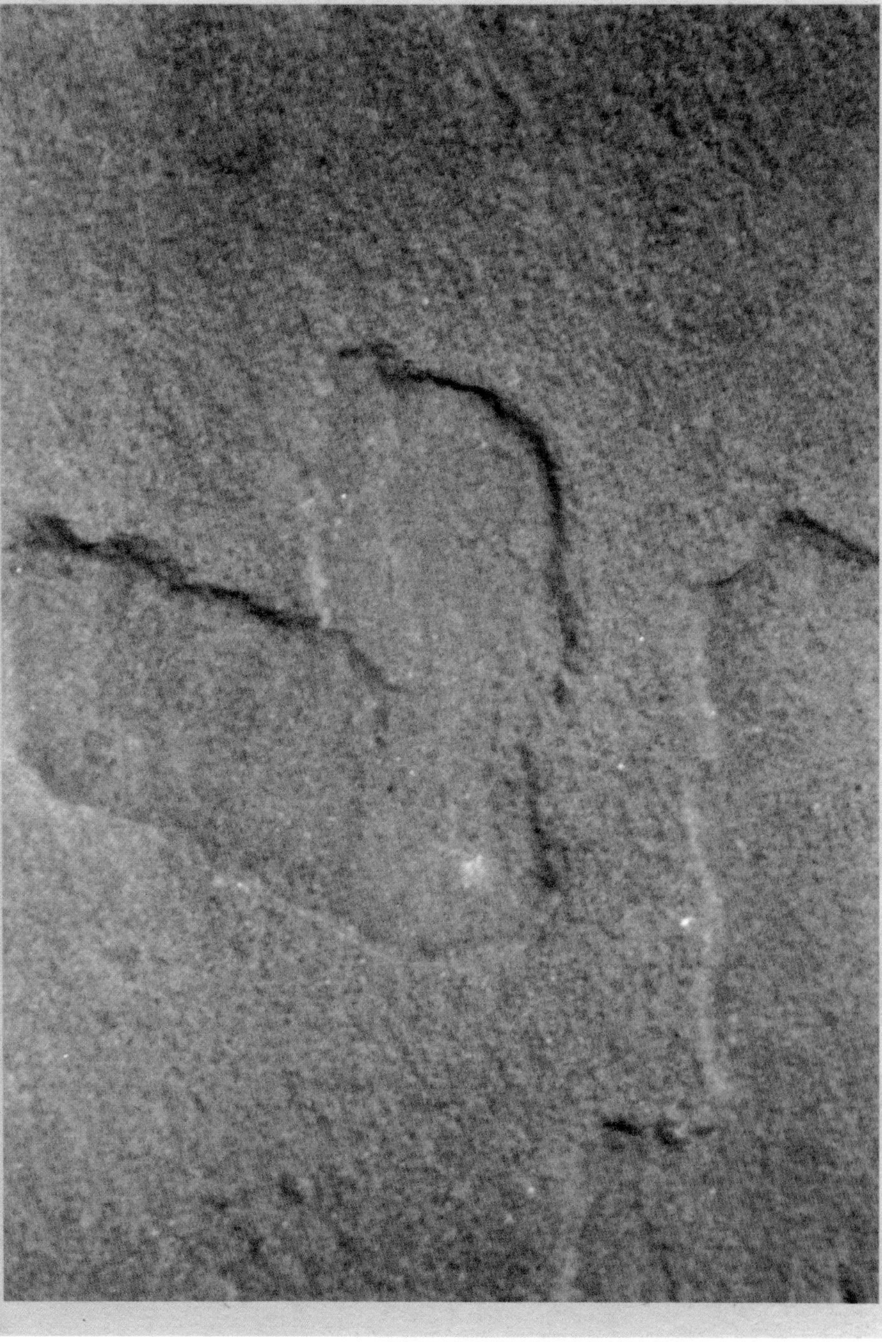

Soar with me on
wings of love.
To places never
before traveled.
Hearts locked,
weaving through time,
May our love never unravel.

I can barely describe it.
It is one of those things that
can't quite be put into words.
It is a feeling.
One that is overpowering and
dominant.
It creeps from behind and
grabs you,
Then you're caught, a slave.
It is with you at all times,
pestering and tormenting.
Now you are no longer able to think.
The feeling has taken over.
It warms and nourishes you,
building and growing constantly
inside you.
You are no longer yourself.
The feeling of love has prevailed.

Morgan Fine

The Passionate Shepherd to His Love

Come live with me, and be my love;
And we will all the pleasures prove
That hills and valleys, dales and fields,
Woods, or steepy mountain yields.

And we will sit upon the rocks,
Seeing the shepherds feed their flocks
By shallow rivers, to whose falls
Melodious birds sing madrigals.

And I will make thee beds of roses,
And a thousand fragrant posies;
A cap of flowers, and a kirtle
Embroidered all with leaves of myrtle;

A gown made of the finest wool
Which from our pretty lambs we pull;
Fair-lined slippers for the cold,
With buckles of the purest gold;

A belt of straw and ivy-buds,
With coral clasps and amber studs;
And if these pleasures may thee move,
Come live with me, and be my love.

The shepherd-swains shall dance and sing
For thy delight each May morning;
If these delights thy mind may move,
Then live with me, and be my love.

—Christopher Marlowe (1564–1593)

Let Me Not to the Marriage of True Minds

Let me not to the marriage of true minds
Admit impediments. Love is not love
Which alters when it alteration finds
Or bends with the remover to remove.
O, no! It is an ever-fixed mark
That looks on tempests and is never shaken;
It is the star to every wand'ring bark,
Whose worth's unknown, although his height be taken.
Love's not Time's fool, though rosy lips and cheeks
Within his bending sickle's compass come.
Love alters not with his brief hours and weeks,
But bears it out even to the edge of doom.
  If this be error and upon me proved,
  I never writ, nor no man ever loved.

—William Shakespeare (1564–1616)

Desire

Blood red they sit beside me,
Wet and ripe
Evoking sensual desire.
Wanton red lips,
Lusting with love,
Thirsting, intriging, inviting.
Mixed together in earthly richness,
Heavenly tastes,
Nothing wasted.
Blood red they sit beside me.

Sonnet Number 51

Thus can my love excuse the slow offense
Of my dull bearer, when from thee I speed—
From where thou art, why should I haste me thence?
Till I return, of posting is no need.
O what excuse will my poor beast then find,
When swift extremity can seem but slow?
Then should I spur, though mounted on the wind—
In wingèd speed no motion shall I know.
Then can no horse with my desire keep pace;
Therefore desire, of perfect'st love being made,
Shall neigh, no dull flesh in his fiery race,
But love, for love, thus shall excuse my jade—
Since from thee going he went wilful slow,
Towards thee I'll run, and give him leave to go.

William Shakespeare
(23 April 1564 - 23 April 1616)

Love

I beg to you,
listen to me.
You are still young,
there may be a chance.
Watch yourself, keep in control,
morning, noon and night
maintain the watch.
It is sneaky, it is clever
and it will stop at nothing.
It wants to conquer you,
so it can occupy your being,
and seep through your veins.
It is a deceptive scoundrel,
so watch out for love.

Morgan Fine

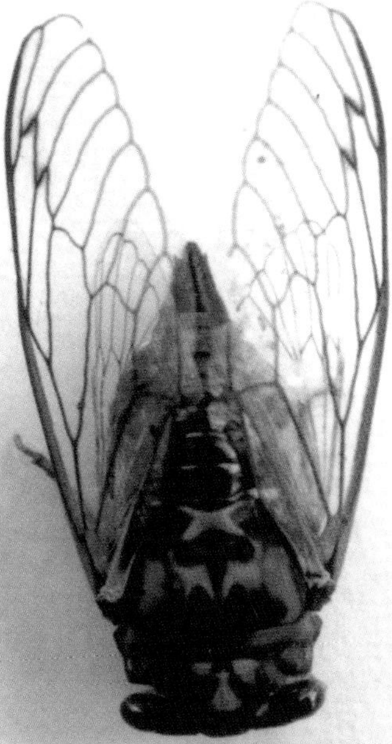

One word frees us of all the weight and pain of life: that word is love.

Sophocles
c. 496 - 406

The Sound of the Sea

The sea awoke at midnight from its sleep,
And round the pebbly beaches far and wide
I heard the first wave of the rising tide
Rush onward with uninterrupted sweep;
A voice out of the silence of the deep,
A sound mysteriously multiplied
As of a cataract from the mountain's side,
Or roar of winds upon a wooded steep.
So comes to us at times, from the unknown
An inaccessible solitudes of being,
The rushing of the sea-tides of the soul;
And inspirations, so that we deem our own,
Are some divine foreshadowing and foreseeing
Of things beyond our reason control.

Henry Wadsworth Longfellow
[27 February 1807 -24 March 1882]

It is a wonderful
seasoning of all
enjoyments to think
of those we love.

Molière
(1621 - 1673)

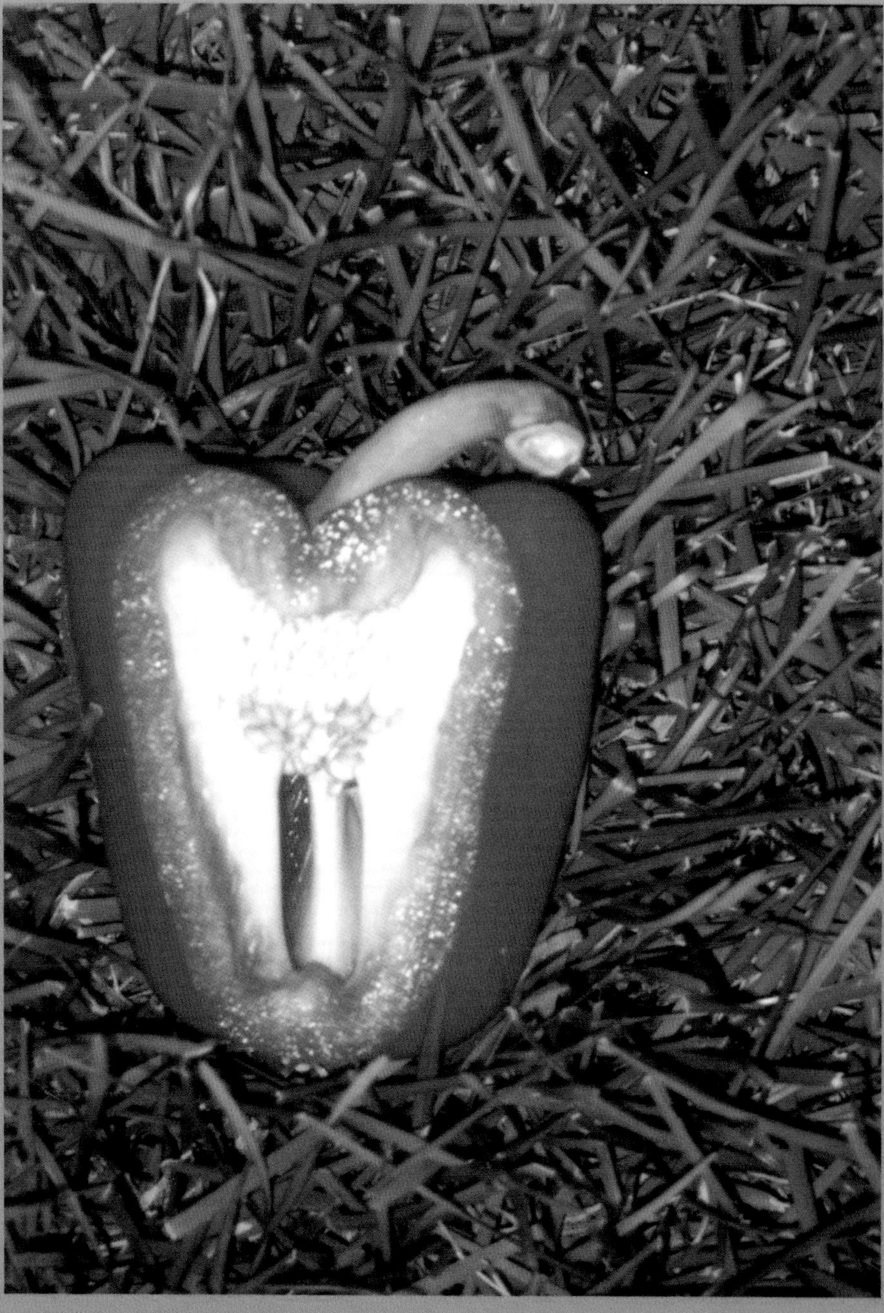

Colors are the smiles of nature...
They are her laughs, as in flowers.

Leigh Hunt
(1784 - 1859)

**Come forth into the light of things,
let nature be your teacher.**

William Wordsworth
(1770 - 1850)

There is no remedy for love
but to love more.

Henry David Thoreau
(1817 - 1862)

Clarity of mind means clarity
of passion, too: this is why a
clear and great mind loves
ardently and sees distinctly
what it loves.

Blaise Pascal
(1623 - 1662)

Keep your love of nature, for that is the true way to understand art and more.

Vincent Van Gogh
(30 March 1853 - 29 July 1890)

All thoughts, all passions,
all delights,
whatever stirs this
mortal frame,
all are but ministers of
love,
and feed his sacred flame.

Samuel Taylor Coleridge
(1772 - 1834)

There is not a sprig of grass that shoots uninteresting to me.

Thomas Jefferson
(13 April 1743 - 4 July 1826)

**Love conquers all things;
let us surrender to love.**

Virgil
17 - 19

How good is man's life, the mere living!
How fit to empty all the heart and the soul and the senses forever to enjoy.

Robert Browning
(7 May 1812 - 1889)

Baby

I'll wrap my arms around your
baby new skin,
and rock you in my arms until
the light grows dim.
I'll keep you close, right by my side,
so we can see eye to eye.
I'll nourish you always and dress
you to the nine.
I'm very proud that you are mine.
Mine to love, to appreciate,
to pamper always and make life great.
You'll be my companion and your soul
I'll let sing.
We'll go exploring and discover
wonderful things.
You're my new baby,
that makes you very dear.
I'm lucky to be with you
as you grow from year to year.

Baby

The creation of a baby,
a miracle, a journey
of love, an attachment
from the heart. Endless joy.

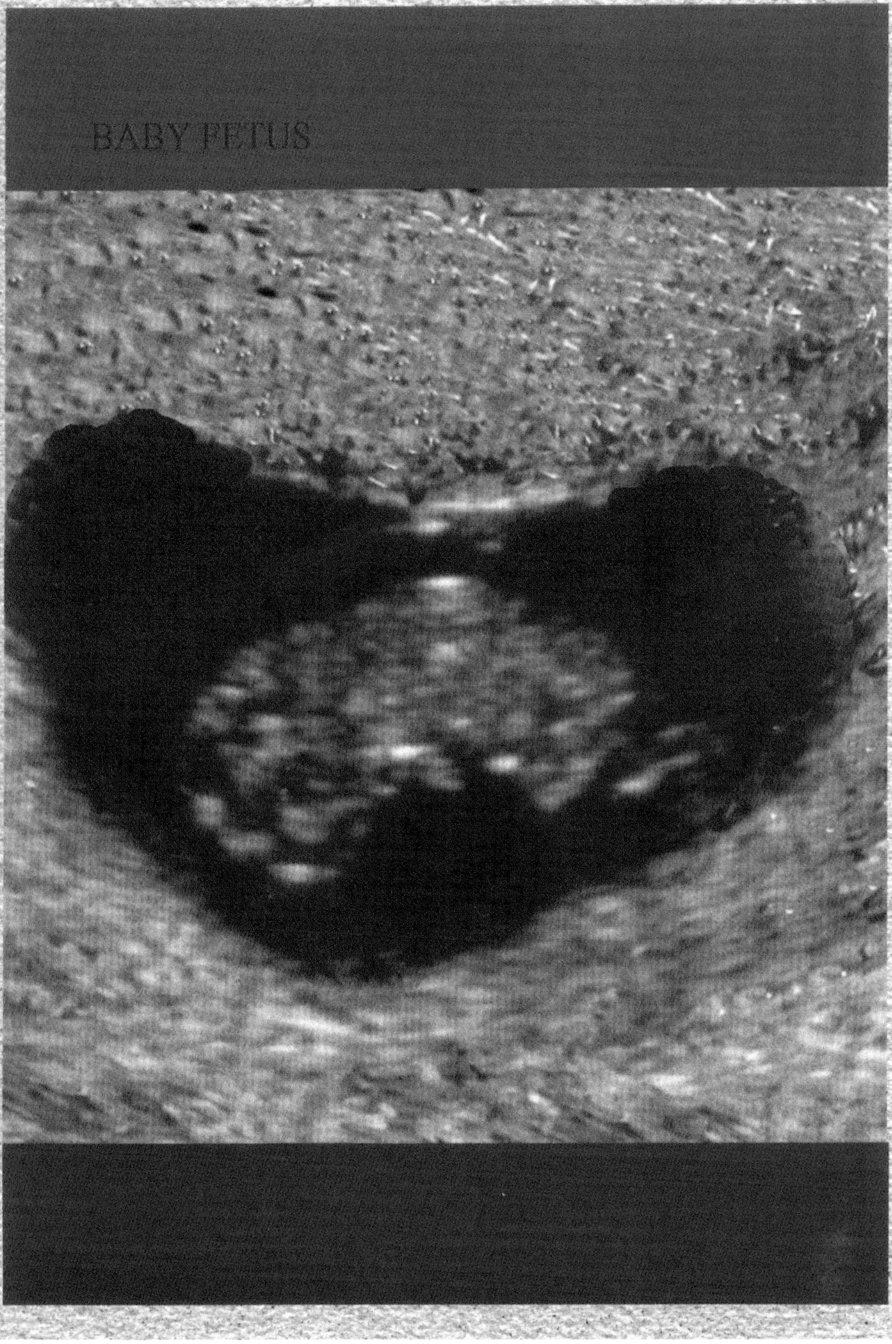
BABY FETUS

Remembering

I planted you in the shape of a birch
  to have your presence near.
To look upon its exquisit form
  and remember my love so dear.
Its dancing leaves captures your laugh,
  the trunk your long, smooth legs.
It comforts, with its cooling shade
  helping me pass the day.
Our love grew deep, like roots reaching
  into the moist earth.
Now you are gone into the unknown,
  yet feeling rebirth.
My memory holds your touch,
  your warmth, your melodious sound.
The beauty, the uniqueness, the essence
  of you abounds.
I planted you in the shape of a birch
  to have your presence near.
To look upon its exquisite form
  and remember my love so dear.

Your radiance
  melts my heart.
I am a puddle
  at your feet,
ready to surround
  you with love.

One touch of nature makes
the whole world kin.

William Shakespeare
(23 April 1564 - 23 April 1616)

Sonnet 47

Betwixt mine eye and heart a league is took,
And each doth good turns now unto the other.
When that mine eye is famish'd for a look,
Or heart in love with sighs himself doth smother;
With my love's picture then my eye doth feast,
And to the painted banquet bids my heart;
Another time mine eye is my heart's guest,
And in his thoughts of love doth share a part;
So, either by thy picture or my love,
Thyself away art resent still with me;
For thou not farther than my thoughts canst move,
And I am still with them and they with thee;
Or, if they sleep, thy picture in my sight
Awakes my heart to heart's and eye's delight.

William Shakespeare
(23 April 1564 - 23 April 1616)

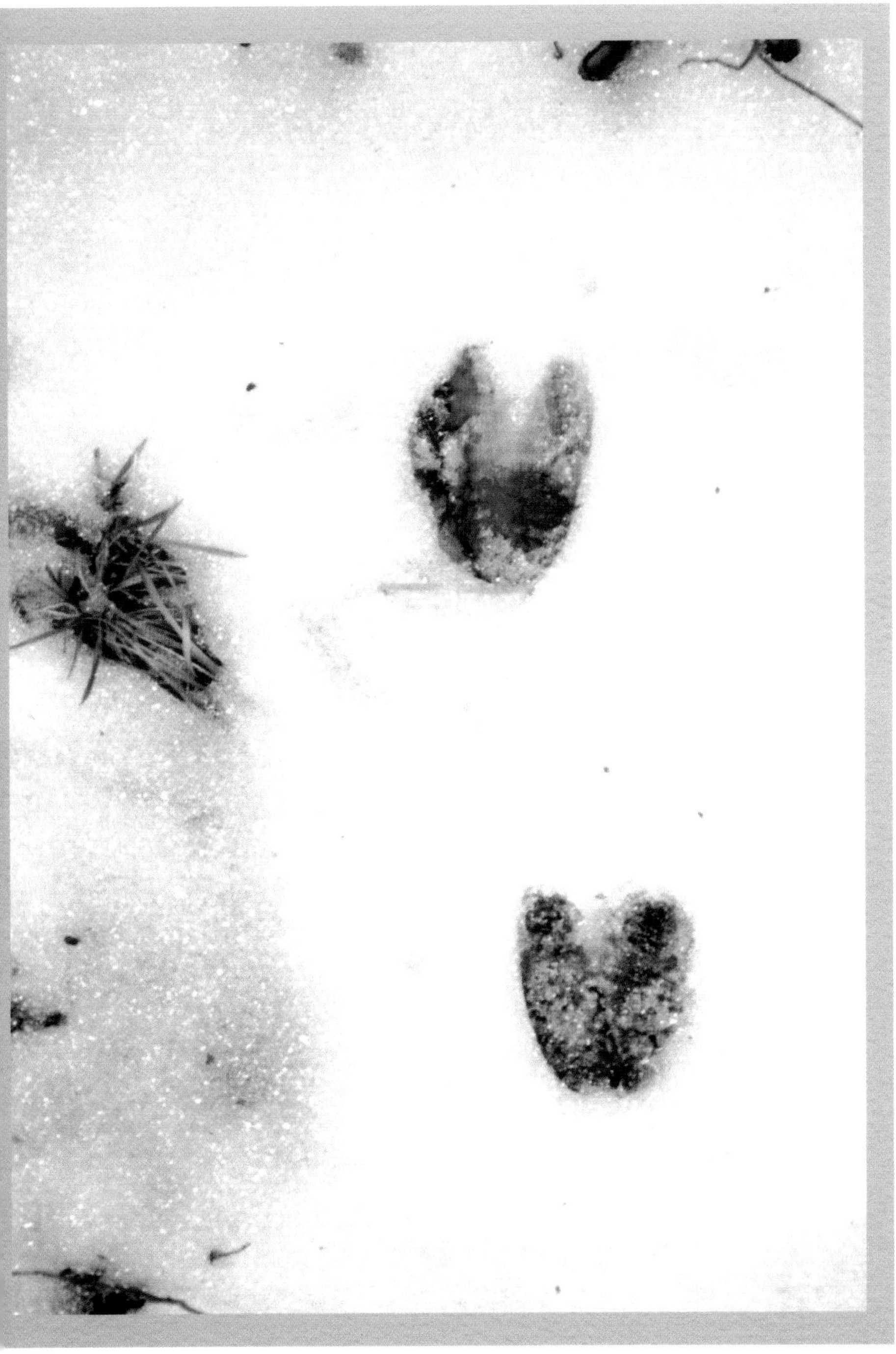

You are rooted in my heart

You are joy and inspiration

You give hope and strength

You are love.

Let not my heart harden,
grow cold and lock.
But expand with love,
as we change
and grow old together.

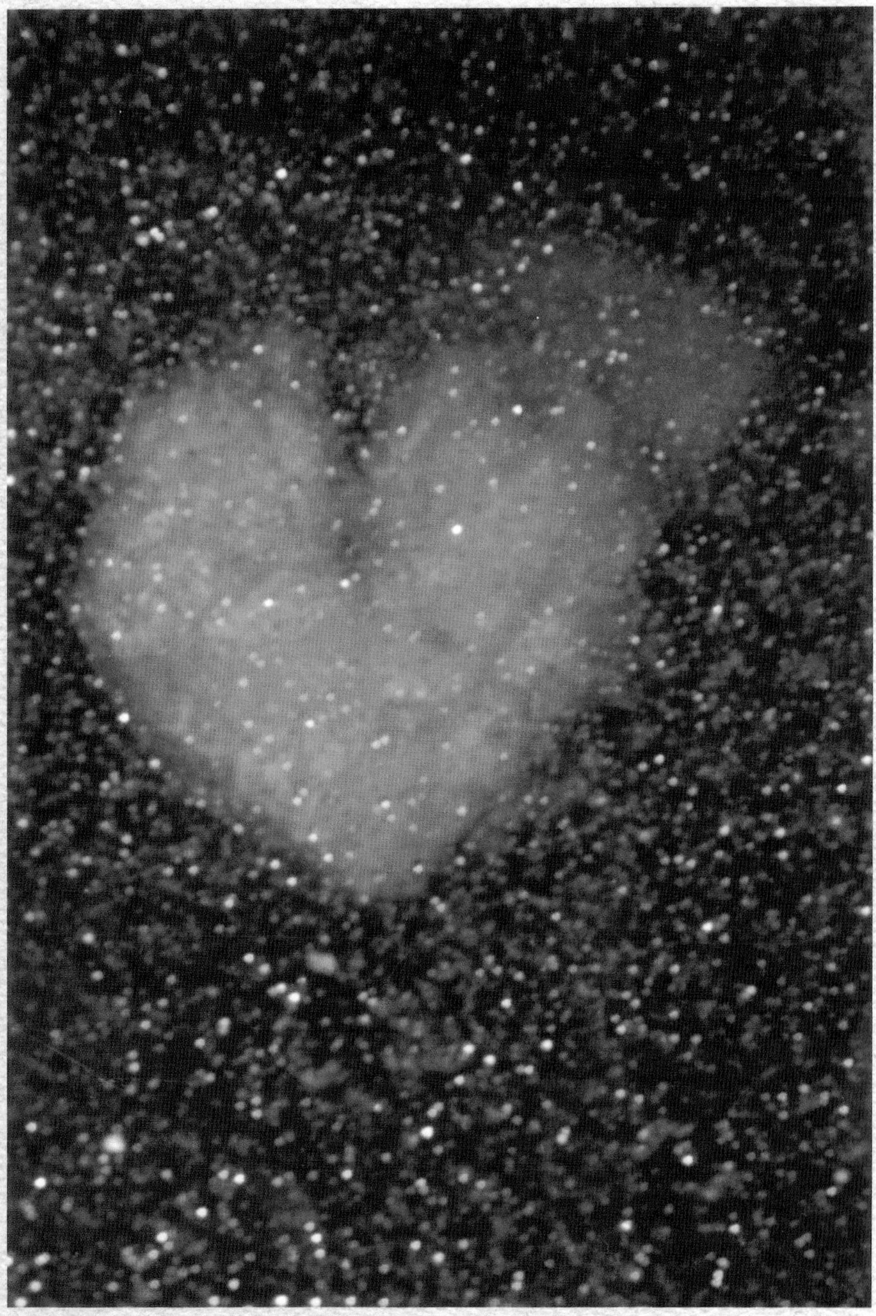

Let me fold you in my arms,
Comfort you and keep you safe.
My love is a blanket surrounding
you with love.

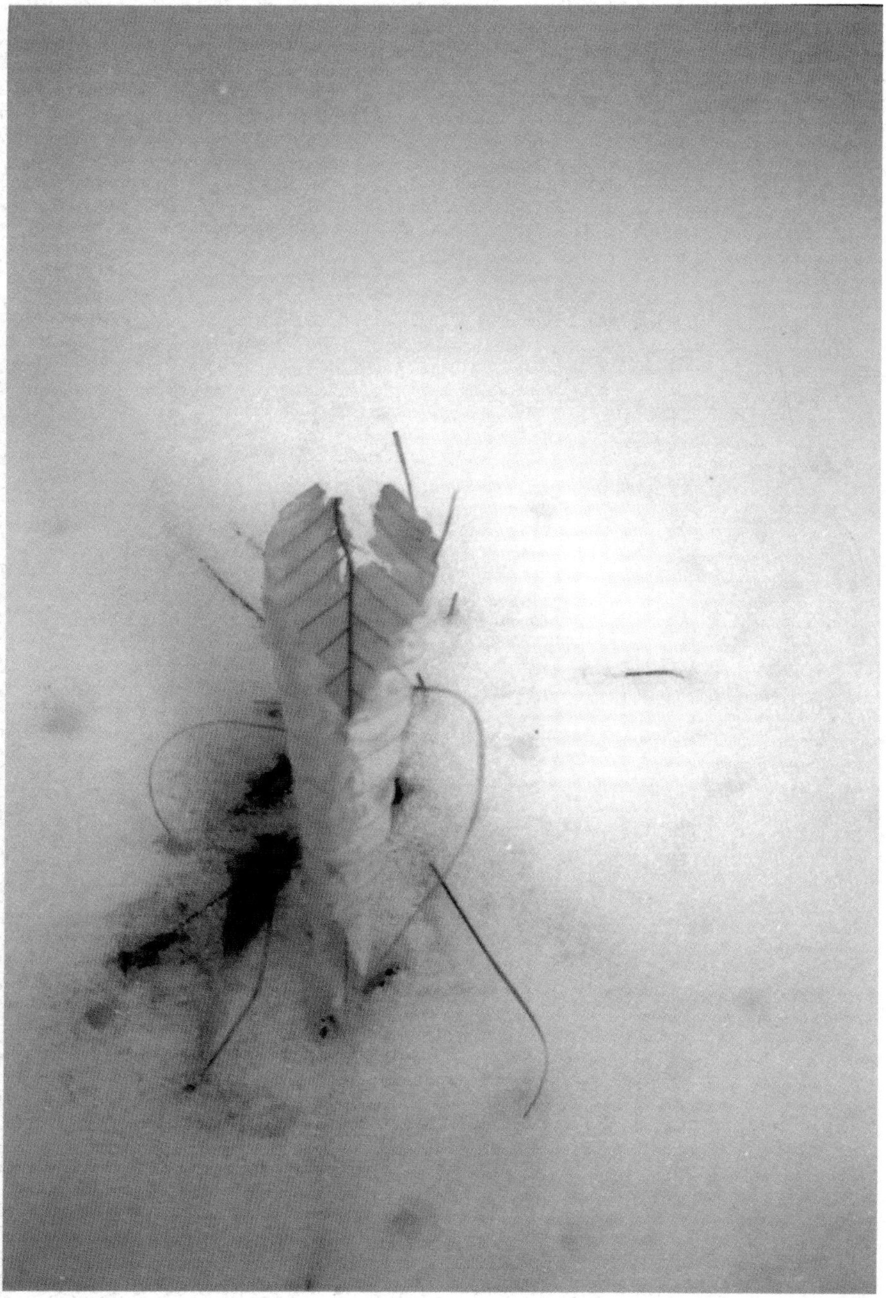

Sonnet 97

How like a winter hath my absence been
From thee, the pleasure of the fleeting year!
What freezings have I felt, what dark days seen!
What old December's bareness every where!
And yet this time removed was summer's time;
The teeming autumn, big with rich increase,
Bearing the wanton burden of the prime,
Like widow'd wombs after their lords' decease.
Yet this abundant issue seem'd to me
But hope of orphans and unfather'd fruit;
For summer and his pleasures wait on thee,
And, thou away, the very birds are mute;
  Or, if they sing, 'tis with so dull a cheer,
  That leaves look pale, dreading the winter's near.

William Shakespeare
(23 April 1564 - 23 April 1616)

A change is coming
It won't be long now
It is inevitable
It cannot be stopped
It will not yield
It is a revolution
It will take over the world
It will fill the hearts of all
It is what drives us all
It is love.

Morgan Fine

Consume me.
Make me part of you.
Let us be together,
Forever on the journey,
Experiencing life as one.

PELE'S WARNING

Wild and torrid my love spews
forth embracing all that is near.
Deceive me,
My heart turns to stone.

Pictured heart photographed in the Kilauea crater on the island of Hawaii.

PELE - Goddess who eats
the land.

Hearts

One heart makes a beat.
Two hearts create a song.

The Symbolic Heart

The heart symbol has for many years been associated with love and the human soul. Long ago, European hunters depicted the heart shape to represent the life-giving organism that they discovered in animals. This shape symbolizing the center of human emotion, continued to be found in various religions and cultures throughout history.

In the middle ages the heart symbolized togetherness, fire and flight.

The Romans and the Greeks associated the heart with sexual love.

The Victorian era loved the shape of the heart, using it to adorn motifs and to give added meaning to written messages.

In the Christian religion, the heart stands for the soul of Jesus. The symbol is often found in cloister decorations and stained glass windows.

The Egyptian AB stands for "Heart Soul" and very closely resembles the Christian iconographs seen in stained glass windows. "The story of the AB tells us that one of the Egyptian seven souls was suppose to come directly from the mother's heart, in the form of holy luna blood and would descend to the womb and take the shape of the child."

An interesting explanation of the heart symbol is connected to erotic love and a ruined city in North Africa. In the 7th century B.C. a worthy plant called silphium was commercially traded in the city-state of Cyrene. This trade made Cyrene one of the wealthiest cities in Africa. The plant was special because it was believed to be an effective means of birth control. The seedpod of the silphium plant is shaped like a stylized heart and is found on the coinage of Cyrene.

Today the heart symbol is still seen in abundance. The symbol is used in jewelry, writing, music and art. The simplicity of this symbol will probably continue to convey its message forever.

To me walking is a source of joy. I find it to be a time of contemplation and renewal of energy. Walking creates in me a source of completeness gathered from the rhythm of movement and a wonder of nature. I find walking to be a time for solving problems and creating new ideas. Walking adds grace and meaning to life.

Sally Fine

"Love"

(Webster's II, New College Dictionary)

Noun:

- An intense attraction to another person based mainly on sexual desire.
- The deep tenderness, affection, and concern felt for a person with whom one has or wishes to have a relationship based on sexual attraction.
- The object of such an attraction: BELOVED.
- Intense sexual passion.

Transitive Verb :

- To feel love for.
- To caress or embrace.

Intransitive Verb:

- To feel affection or experience sexual desire for another.

Dedicated to my family.
I give you my hearts.

ACKNOWLEDGEMENTS

My thanks to Loren, at http://www.heartsmith.com/heart history.html, for giving me permission to use the information on her website.

All material not credited to author was written by Sally Fine.